DATE DUE		
	T9		

Beginning BASEBALL

Coach Don Geng, Coach Steve Scherber, and the following athletes were photographed for this book:

A.J. Capewell,
Matt Cavanaugh,
John Dittberner,
Ben Doran,
Blake Dotson,
Christian Edwards,
Mike Griffin,
Brandon Hammergren,
Kathryn Hetherington,
Michael Honsa,
Jay Johnson,
Mike Killeen,
Dan Lewer,
Tony Liuzzi,
Melissa Peterson,
Dave Shelley,
Andy Williams,
Rob Worthington.

Beginning BASEBALL

Julie Jensen

Adapted from Don Geng's
Fundamental Baseball

Photographs by Andy King

Lerner Publications Company • Minneapolis

Library of Congress Cataloging-in-Publication Data

Jensen, Julie, 1957–
Beginning baseball / Julie Jensen ; adapted from Don Geng's Fundamental baseball ; photographs by Andy King.
p. cm. — (Beginning sports)
Includes bibliographical references and index.
Summary: Introduces the fundamental techniques of baseball.
ISBN 0–8225–3505–X (alk. paper)
1. Baseball—Juvenile literature. [1. Baseball.] I. Geng, Don. Fundamental baseball. II. King, Andy, ill. III. Title. IV. Series.
GV867.5.J46 1995
796.357—dc20 95–11981

Manufactured in the United States of America

1 2 3 4 5 6 HP 00 99 98 97 96 95

Photo Acknowledgments

Photographs are reproduced with the permission of: pp. 7, 13 (top), Toronto Blue Jays; pp. 9, 10 (top), Independent Picture Service; p. 10 (bottom), Courtesy of the Boston Public Library, Print Department; pp.11 (both), 13 (bottom), National Baseball Hall of Fame and Museum, Cooperstown, N.Y.; p. 12, John Doman/St. Paul Pioneer Press; p. 25, Gregory Drezdzon/Seattle Mariners.

Contents

A Note From Paul Molitor

Since I began playing at the age of five, baseball has given me a great life. I have been on teams that were St. Paul (Minnesota) City Champs at St. Luke's Grade School, State Champions at Attucks Brooks American Legion and Cretin High School, Big Ten Champs at the University of Minnesota, and World Champions for the Toronto Blue Jays. But more important than all of these championships have been the great friends, experiences, and memories.

Always give your best effort whenever you play baseball, whether it's at the playground or at a beautiful diamond. You have to believe in yourself, like the early 1900s player Wee Willie Keeler did. Only 5 feet, 4 inches tall and 140 pounds, Willie still has the fifth highest lifetime batting average in the history of major league baseball. You have to believe that nothing will stop you—not size, not background, not coaching, not equipment.

Is believing in yourself easy? It wasn't for me. I remember crying, sulking, and going off by myself when I had a bad game or made a bad play at a crucial time. How can you avoid these negative, wasteful emotions?

Set goals, long term and short term. Commit yourself to the idea that you will work harder than anyone. You will listen better, practice the details, and never let yourself get discouraged. Set short-term

goals like, "I'll get a hit next time," or "I'll take 50 extra swings in my basement."

If you're lucky, you'll have as many great coaches as I did, and a parent or another family member who encourages and supports you. However, you may not be so lucky as to have everything go your way. Don't let this stop you. Great players have come from the most disadvantaged backgrounds to become Hall of Fame players. Who knows? You may be the next one!

Finally, play hard, but play cleanly and within the rules of the game. Play and practice wholeheartedly, with as much enthusiasm as you have.

Paul Molitor
Most Valuable Player
1993 World Series

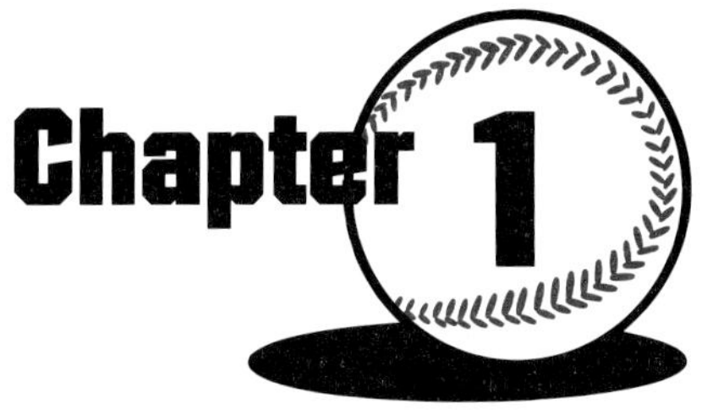

How This Game Got Started

Baseball has seen many changes throughout its history. More has remained the same, however, than has changed.

There have always been two teams playing on a large field. A baseball field has always had four bases.

The teams always take turns trying to hit a ball with a bat. One player tries to hit a ball thrown by a player on the fielding team. If the batter hits the ball, he or she runs and tries to touch all the bases. Once a player has safely touched all the bases, his or her team scores a run. The players on the team in the field try to keep the batter from scoring runs.

This picture is from Robin Carver's 1834 *Book of Sports*. It shows children playing a game like baseball.

No one knows for sure where or when baseball began. It may have come from an old English game called *rounders.* In rounders, a player also hit a ball with a bat and ran around four bases. The players in the field threw the ball at the runner. If the ball hit the runner, he or she couldn't score a run.

Alexander Cartwright

American colonists in the 1700s played rounders, but they called it "base ball." Their game was played by different rules in different areas. Some players in New York City made a big rule change in the 1830s or 1840s. They stopped throwing the ball at the runner. Instead, they held the ball in their hands and touched the runner. Touching the runner this way was

Alexander Cartwright's Base Ball Club of New York was called the Knickerbocker Nine.

called making a **tag**, or tagging the runner. We still use that term.

Alexander Cartwright formed a club called the Knickerbocker Base Ball Club of New York in 1845. His club was just for playing baseball. He also wrote a rule book for the sport. In his rule book, players made a **putout** by tagging a runner.

Baseball became more popular during and after the Civil War. Northern soldiers taught the game to soldiers from all over the country. They played baseball during breaks in the fighting.

The Cincinnati Red Stockings in 1869 became the first team to pay its players. That made the players professionals. The National League began in 1876 with eight professional teams. The American League was formed in 1901.

Women, African Americans, and Hispanics are also a part of baseball's history. Women's teams began in the 1870s at some colleges. During World War II, women played in the All American Girls Professional Baseball League. The league ended after the war.

Babe Ruth had the record for home runs in a career (714) . . .

. . . until Hank Aaron hit his 715th home run in 1974.

The Colorado Silver Bullets are a minor league team made up of women.

Black players played in the Negro Leagues during professional baseball's early days. In 1947 Jackie Robinson became the first black man to play in the major leagues. He played for the Brooklyn Dodgers. He was the National League Most Valuable Player in 1949. Jackie Robinson led the way for thousands of other black players to play in the major leagues.

Many Hispanic ballplayers have played in the major leagues in the United States. Roberto Clemente was a great player for the Pittsburgh Pirates in the 1960s and 1970s. He was the 11th player in baseball to get 3,000 hits in his career.

Baseball is played and enjoyed all over the world. Canada, Mexico, Cuba, the Dominican Republic, Puerto Rico, Nicaragua, and Japan have rich baseball traditions.

Roberto Alomar helped the Toronto Blue Jays win two World Series.

Ty Cobb was a star in the early days of organized baseball.

Markwort

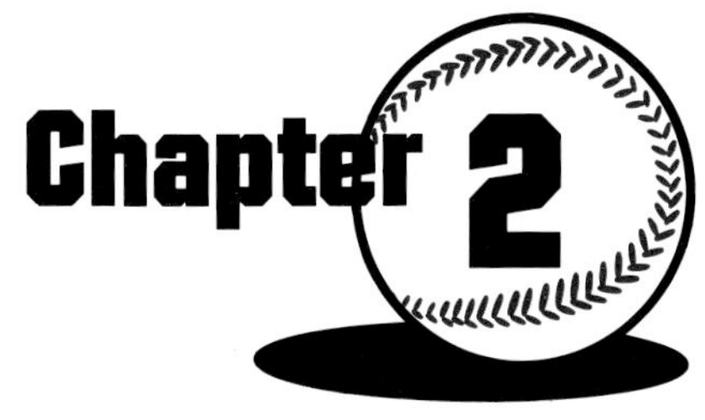

BASICS

Equipment

To play baseball, you need a ball, a bat, and a glove.

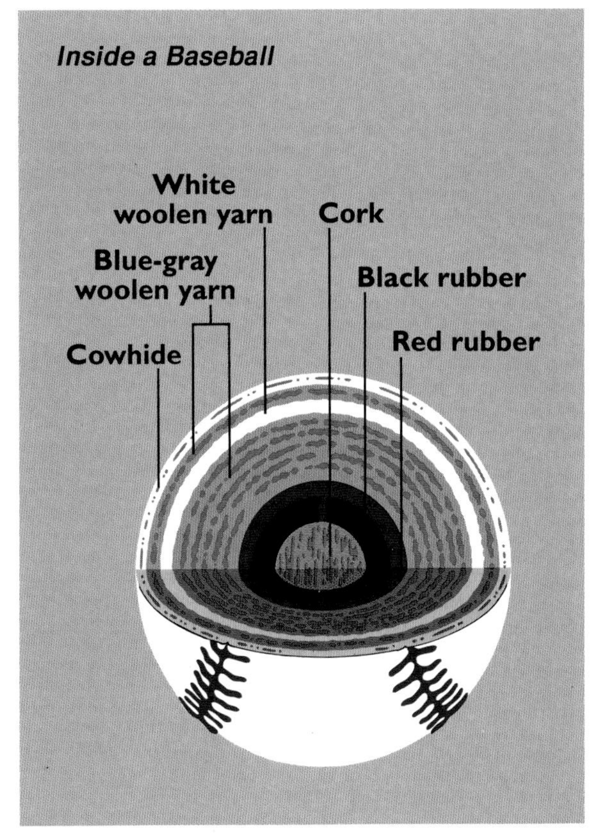

• *The Ball*

Baseballs were once homemade items. People twisted yarn into a ball and covered it with leather. Now, baseballs are made by machines.

An official baseball is 9 to 9¼ inches around. It weighs 5 to 5¼ ounces. A small cork center is covered by two layers of rubber. Three layers of yarn are wrapped around the rubber. The white cover is stitched with heavy red thread.

● *The Bat*

A bat is a long, smooth piece of wood or aluminum. Youth, high school, and college players use aluminum bats because they don't break. Wooden bats are used in professional baseball.

A bat can't be longer than 42 inches and it can't be wider than 2¼ inches at its widest point. A rubber or leather grip covers the handle of a bat. There is a knob at the end of the handle. The part of the bat that hits the ball is called the barrel.

Most hitters think that the heavier the bat is, the harder it will hit the ball. Good hitters know that the lighter the bat is, the quicker the batter's swing will be. The quicker the batter's swing is, the harder he or she will hit the ball.

● *The Glove*

Catchers need special gloves called mitts. Infielders need small gloves so that they can quickly throw the ball. Outfielders and first basemen need big gloves to give them more range.

● *Other Equipment*

A baseball player wears a hard plastic cap when batting. It's called a batting helmet. A batting helmet protects the batter from a pitched ball. A batting helmet also protects a player from a thrown ball while he or she is running the bases. Batting helmets are required in all leagues.

Many baseball players also wear spiked shoes, called cleats, to improve their running. Some also wear a tight-fitting glove when they are batting. This batting glove helps the batter grip the bat better.

Baseball Gloves

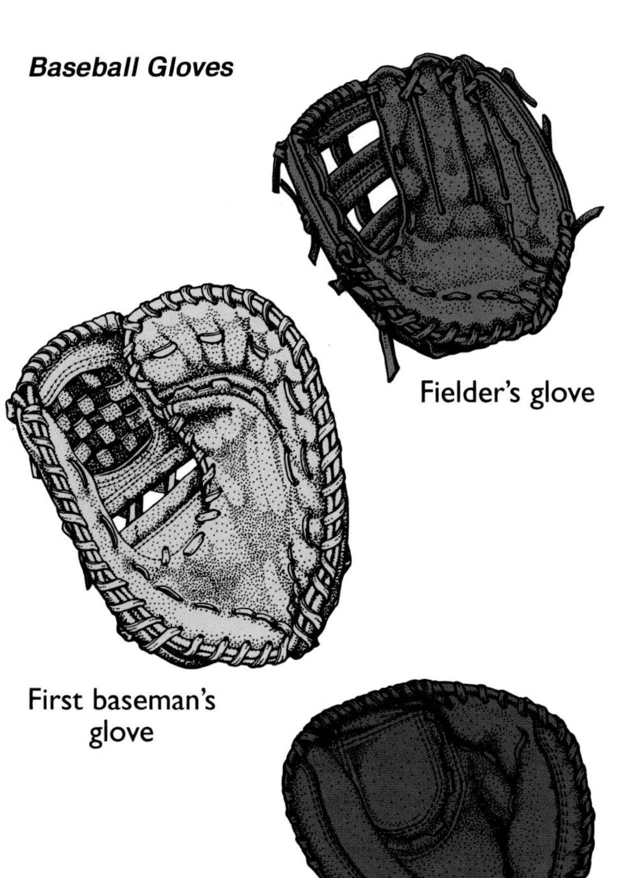

Fielder's glove

First baseman's glove

Catcher's mitt

The Field

A baseball field has an infield, an outfield, and foul territory. The infield is a square area, usually dirt, with a base at each corner. The infield looks like a diamond from behind home plate. That's why baseball fields are often called *diamonds.*

The outfield is a grassy area from the first, second, and third bases to the fence around the field.

The infield and outfield are fair territory. Foul territory is the area outside the foul lines. The foul lines are marked with white chalk.

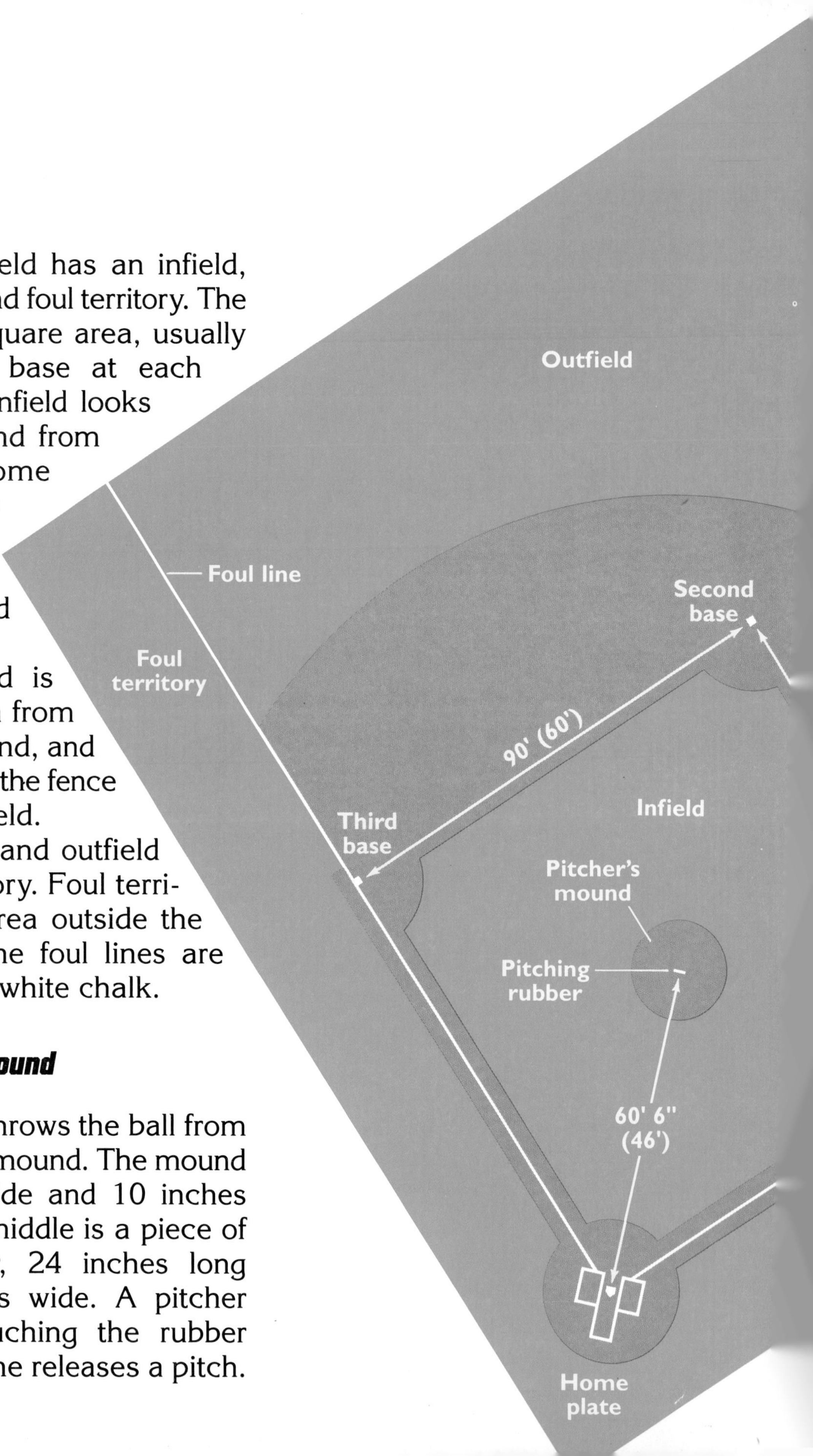

• *Pitcher's Mound*

The pitcher throws the ball from the pitcher's mound. The mound is 18 feet wide and 10 inches high. In the middle is a piece of white rubber, 24 inches long and 6 inches wide. A pitcher must be touching the rubber when he or she releases a pitch.

• *The Bases*

First, second, and third bases are white canvas bags filled with sand. The bases are 15 inches square and 3 to 5 inches thick.

Home plate is a five-sided piece of white rubber. The part of home plate that is nearest the infield is 17 inches wide. Home plate narrows to a point on the side away from the infield.

A rectangle, 6 feet by 4 feet, is marked with chalk on each side of home plate. These areas are called the **batter's box**. A batter must be standing in the batter's box when the pitch is thrown.

The measurements for Little League play are shown in parentheses ( ).

Foul line

90' (60')

First base

Foul territory

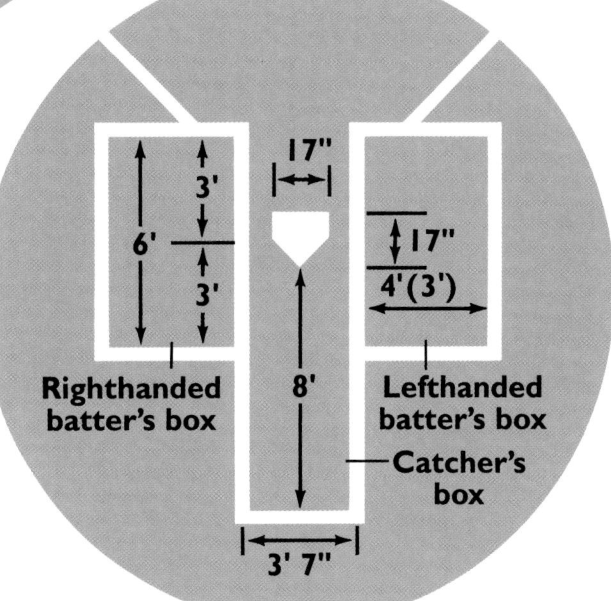

Home Plate Area

The Rules

The visiting team bats first in the game. Each team has one turn at bat each **inning.** A baseball game is six, seven, or nine innings long, unless the score is tied. If that happens, more innings are played until one team wins. If the home team is ahead in the last inning, it doesn't bat.

The pitcher tries to throw the ball through the **strike zone**. The strike zone is an imaginary rectangle that is as wide as home plate. The strike zone goes from the batter's armpits to his or her knees.

A pitch is a **strike** if the batter swings at the ball and misses it. A pitch is also a strike if the batter doesn't swing at it but the umpire says the pitch was in the strike zone. A ball hit to foul territory is also a strike unless the batter already has two strikes. When a batter has three strikes, he or she has made an **out**—a **strikeout**. A team gets three outs each inning.

A **ball** is called when the batter doesn't swing at a pitch and the umpire rules that the ball was outside the strike zone. If a batter gets four balls, he or she goes to first base on a **base on balls,** or walk.

If the batter hits the ball in fair territory, the fielders try to catch the ball. If a fielder catches the ball in the air, the batter is out. But if the ball isn't caught before it hits the ground, the hitter becomes a baserunner.

A baserunner's goal is to touch all the bases, starting at first base and ending at home plate. Safely reaching home plate scores one run for the baserunner's team. The fielders try to keep baserunners from scoring runs.

Once a runner has reached a base, he or she can't be tagged out while still touching the base. The runner can remain on a base until the next batter gets a walk or a **hit**. Once the ball is in play again, the baserunner can try to go to the next base.

A baserunner is tagged out if he or she isn't on a base and is touched by a fielder who is holding the ball. A baserunner can also be put out by a **force-out**. If a fielder has the ball and touches first base before the baserunner does, the runner is forced out. A runner also can be forced out at the other bases if there are runners on all the bases behind him or her.

A single is a hit that lets the batter get to first base safely. If the batter gets to second base on a hit, that hit is a double. If the batter reaches third base, the hit is a triple. If the batter reaches home plate on the hit, the batter has hit a **home run**.

Sometimes a player hits the ball and a fielder makes a mistake. For example, a fielder might throw the ball over the first baseman's head. In that case, the batter reaches base on an **error**, not a hit.

There's another way a batter can reach first base safely. If the fielders decided to force out a baserunner instead of putting out the batter, the batter reaches base on a **fielder's choice**.

If the fielders put out two baserunners with one play, they have made a **double play**. Often, a double play is made when a baserunner is on first base and the batter hits the ball to the infield. The fielders force out the runner at second base and get the ball to first base before the batter gets there.

The Positions

Each team uses nine fielders when it isn't batting. Each fielder has an area of the field to cover. The pitcher covers the mound. The catcher covers home plate.

The first baseman, second baseman, and third baseman all play near their bases. The shortstop plays between the second and third bases. These four players are infielders.

The outfielders are spread across the outfield. The leftfielder is behind the area between second and third base. The centerfielder plays behind second base. The rightfielder is behind the area between the first and second bases.

P

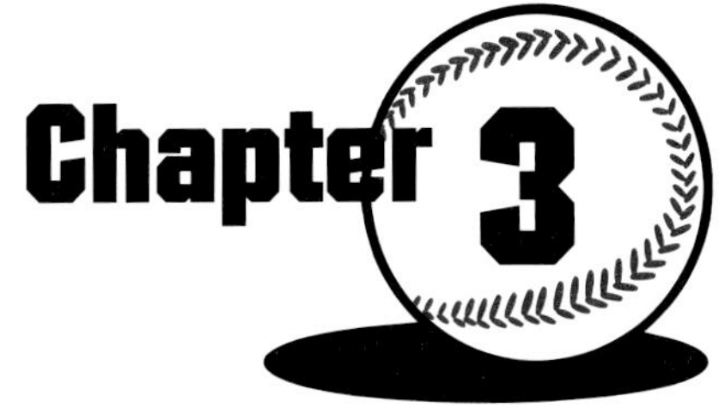

FIELDING

There are four things a baseball player must do: Field the ball, throw the ball, hit the ball, and run. Learning how to do these things will take time and effort. The best players say that they never quit trying to improve.

To be a good fielder, learn to catch without a glove. Cradle the ball. Don't let it slap against your hands. Pretend your hands are made of glass. If the ball hits your hands too hard, your hands will break.

Ken Griffey Jr. played on the Seattle Mariners with his dad for one season. Ken is an outstanding outfielder.

Dave and Andy are practicing with their bare hands and a tennis ball. First, Dave runs five steps away from his coach. The coach lobs the ball ahead of Dave. Dave looks over his shoulder. He sees the ball and catches it. Then it's Andy's turn.

After both boys have caught 10 balls, they use their gloves and a baseball. Don't reach out your glove until the last second before you catch the ball. Running with your glove hand out slows you down.

Fielding Ground Balls

A **ground ball** hits the ground before a fielder can catch it. Matt and Katy are fielding ground balls.

• *The Stance*

Matt waits for the batter to hit the ball. He bends forward and puts his hands on his knees. His legs are set wider apart than his shoulders. This gives Matt better balance and keeps him close to the ground. His weight is on the balls of his feet.

• *The Glove*

Matt's glove is open and on the ground. Keep your glove touching the ground so that the ball can't go under it. Keep your arm out in front of you so that you can see the ball go into the glove.

• *Moving to the Ball*

Katy runs to the ball quickly. Then she slows down. She spreads her legs to get closer to the ground.

● *Fielding the Ball*

Katy uses both hands to field the grounder. She watches the ball go into her glove. Katy's top hand acts like a garbage can cover. As the ball enters her glove, her throwing hand covers the ball. Katy will be able to throw the ball quickly because her throwing hand is already touching the ball. Practice doing this in slow motion without a ball.

Fielding Fly Balls

When catching a **fly ball** or a **pop fly,** remember to cushion the ball. Try to catch the ball above your head whenever you can. That way you can watch the ball land in your glove. If you fumble the ball, you have another chance to catch it before it hits the ground. Missy's gloved fingers point up because she is catching a fly ball above her waist.

Catching a ball below your waist with your fingers pointing up is awkward. If you have to catch a fly ball below your waist, as Ben is doing in the photograph above, point your gloved fingers down.

When you have to run to catch a fly ball, run on the balls of your feet. Don't run on your heels. Running on your heels makes your body bounce.

THROWING

After you field the ball, you often must throw it. When you throw, be sure your shoulders are level. Point your lead shoulder directly at your target. Step directly toward that target.

● *The Grip*

A good throw begins with the right grip. Place your index and middle finger ½ to 1 inch across the baseball's big seams. (You may hold the ball with three fingers also.) Grip the ball loosely with your fingertips. Put your thumb underneath and toward the middle of the ball. The ball should be on the side of your thumb, not the pad of your thumb tip.

• The Stance

Katy's weight is on the ball of her back foot. Her back leg is bent. She will drive forward off her back leg toward the target.

Katy's shoulders are level. Her shoulders aim the ball. If her shoulders slope upward, her throw will be a high one. If Katy's shoulders aim to the right or left of the target, the ball will go in that direction.

Katy holds her glove at shoulder level. It's about 12 inches from her shoulder. Her elbow is down and her wrist is bent.

• *Cocking the Arm*

Katy's arm is behind her. Her palm is down and her elbow is slightly above her shoulder. The farther Katy can reach backward without her elbow locking, the more power she will have. Katy is in the *eagle position*. Think of the long wingspan of an eagle. If your throws aren't fast, your arm is probably only extending back like a duck's.

Arm Care

Before you throw, stretch. Do exercises like toe touches, arm circles, and jumping jacks. Warm up your muscles by jogging.

Then start to throw with a partner. Lob the ball half the distance from the plate to the mound. Gradually get farther apart until you're throwing from the plate to second base.

Don't throw hard early in the season. Start slowly and build your strength. Always keep your arm warm when you are throwing. Cold muscles are more likely to be hurt. In cool weather, wear a sweatshirt.

Stop throwing any time your shoulder, elbow, or wrist starts to hurt. If you do get a sore arm, rest it.

• The Release

Katy keeps most of her weight on her back leg. She keeps her shoulders level. Her palm has rotated. It was facing the ground. Now it's facing the sky.

Katy steps forward 6 to 12 inches with her front foot. As she steps toward her target, Katy's front hip rotates so that her knee and foot point to the target.

As Katy's front foot hits the ground, her arm moves forward. Katy's elbow, level or slightly above her shoulder, leads her arm.

When you throw, keep the ball just higher than your head. If you drop your elbow, the ball will drop below head height. Then you will push the ball. Your throw will be high and slow.

Katy whips the ball ahead of her elbow and snaps her wrist. She releases the ball when her arm is fully extended.

For an outfield throw, a player may need more power. The *crow hop* helps a player create more power for a throw.

Matt demonstrates a crow hop. He hops on his back foot. Matt releases the ball as he lands on his front foot. He steps directly toward the target with his front foot.

• The Follow-Through

Katy's throwing hand ends up on the outside of her forward knee. Her back is bent a little bit. Katy's back leg has swung forward. Her back foot ends up slightly ahead of her front foot.

Throwing Practice

Practice your throwing motion 25 times a day in slow motion. When you practice, use all the muscles in your feet, legs, sides, back, shoulders, arm, and wrist. Your arm will stay strong and healthy if you use all these muscles to throw.

Throw as much as you can. Play catch with friends anywhere—away from windows, of course! Throwing a tennis ball against a wall also helps.

Dave and Andy are throwing high, lazy, long throws. This strengthens their arms without hurting them. Remember, stop throwing if you feel sore. You only have one good throwing arm. Take care of it!

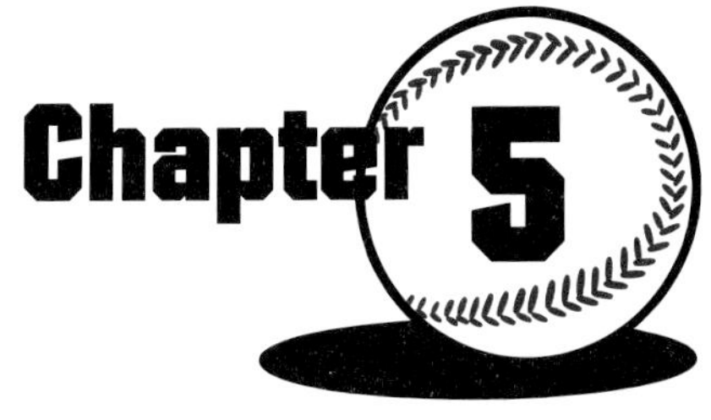

HITTING

Hitting is the toughest part of baseball—and the most fun! View each **at bat** as a challenge. Don't expect a hit every time. If you strike out, don't get discouraged. Concentrate on getting a hit the next time. Try to hit the ball squarely, with as quick a swing as you can.

Have a positive attitude and practice every day. Then you will improve. Work on improving your skills at practice, not in a game.

Set realistic goals. Try to get on base at least once each game, with a walk, error, or hit. Once you reach this goal, every other time on base is a bonus.

Swinging Practice

Practice swinging the bat at imaginary baseballs. Throw the barrel quickly. Keep practicing until the bat feels like it's a part of you.

• The Grip

Dave holds the bat loosely. The bottom three fingers of each hand are relaxed. His finger knuckles (those you use when knocking on a door), not his hand knuckles, line up.

Dave holds the bat firmly, as he would hold a hammer. He doesn't hold the bat tightly. Squeezing the bat too hard slows your swing.

● *The Ready Position*

Dave's feet are slightly farther apart than his shoulders. His weight is on the balls of his feet. Both knees are bent slightly. If Dave looks down, he sees his knees, not his feet.

The bat rests on Dave's shoulder. His top hand is near the top of his back shoulder. When the pitcher starts to throw the ball, Dave lifts the bat. His top hand is even with the top of his back shoulder and over his back toe.

Dave's eyes, shoulders, and elbows are level so he can see the pitch. His head is turned so both eyes look directly at the pitcher. His chin is near his front shoulder. (Turn your head far enough so that your eyes aren't blocked by your nose or your glasses.)

Think of this position that Dave is demonstrating as the *Pete* position. When you swing, you go from the *Pete* position to the *Sweet* position. In the *Sweet* position, your chin is near your back shoulder. Your eyes are looking down the bat's barrel.

• Cocking

To begin his swing, Ben turns his lower body 1 inch so that his back pocket points toward the pitcher. This cocks the front hip and puts his weight on his back foot. As Ben cocks his hips, he moves his hands back 1 to 2 inches.

When you're batting, keep the bat as still as possible when cocking. Don't wave the barrel back and forth. A still bat is called a quiet bat. A quiet bat begins each swing from the same starting point. A bat starting from the same position for each swing results in a consistent swing.

• Striding

Next, Ben lifts his knee about 1 inch. His front foot is on its ball. His heel is slightly raised. Ben takes a short, 1- to 3-inch stride forward with his front foot.

Ben strides directly toward the pitcher. He lands on the ball of his front foot. His swing shifts his weight to his heel. When striding, imagine that you are stepping onto a thin piece of ice. Stepping too hard would send you crashing into the water.

The "Sweet" Position

Ben keeps his eyes on the ball, not the bat. His chin is near his back shoulder. His back elbow is close to his body but his arms are fully extended. Remember, this is the *Sweet* position. You go from *Pete* to *Sweet* when swinging properly.

Ben's hips have rotated like a giant spring uncoiling. His back foot has twisted so that his toe points toward the pitcher. This motion is like squishing a bug. The player who doesn't squish the bug isn't releasing all of his or her power.

Ben's bottom hand and left elbow pull the bat down and directly toward the pitcher. His top hand throws the barrel of the bat toward and through the ball. Ben's top arm extends at contact. When you are swinging, whip the barrel through the ball and keep your hands close to your body.

Practice = Perfection

After you have learned the basics of hitting, there's only one way to become a better hitter. You have to practice, and practice correctly.

Start with this practice routine:

1. *Each day, work on one or two parts of your swing.*
2. *Swing 25 times in slow motion.*
3. *Take 25 good swings. Think about the part of the swing on which you're working. Don't just wave a bat in the air. Imagine yourself in a real game. See yourself hitting pitches in all parts of the strike zone. Feel confident. Feel relaxed.*
4. *Hit 25 balls off a tee. Whiffle balls or tennis balls work.*

By practicing with this plan, your swing will become natural to you. Then, when you're batting in a game, relax and trust what you've practiced.

• *Following Through*

Ben keeps his head still as he follows through. His hands finish up near his front shoulder.

The Mental Game

The players on a team bat in order. That order is called the **lineup**, or the batting order. The head coach, or manager, sets the lineup.

While you are waiting for your turn to bat, study the other team's pitcher. Try to figure out his or her patterns. Are this pitcher's pitches usually high or low? What pitches does this pitcher throw first to a batter?

Have a plan at the plate. Be selective, but be aggressive. Attack every good pitch. Watch the seams of the ball spin. Watch the ball hit your bat. Keep your head down until your follow-through is completed.

Learn how to recognize a **fastball**, a **change-up**, and a **curveball**. If the pitcher is throwing a lot of balls, you can be choosy. Look for the pitch that you can hit best. Your best pitch may be high or low, to the inside or to the outside part of the plate.

With one strike, you can't be as picky. Look for a pitch you can drive, even if it's not in your favorite spot.

Once you get two strikes, focus on hitting the ball somewhere. Don't hope for a walk. Hit the ball and make something happen.

• *Hitting Line Drives*

To raise your **batting average,** try to hit a **line drive** up the middle of the field. The middle is the most open area of the field. The shortstop and second baseman are on either side of second base. The pitcher is often off balance after releasing the ball. The pitcher and infielders don't have much time to field a hard-hit ball.

• *Hitting to All Fields*

To *pull* the ball means to hit it to left field if you are a right-handed hitter or right field if you are lefthanded. To hit the ball to the opposite field means to hit it to right field if you are a righthander. When you can pull the ball or hit it to the opposite field, you can hit to all fields.

Whole-Body Hitting

You are stronger when you use your legs, hips, and back than when you use just your arms and hands. Try to swing on your knees. Notice how little power your arms have by themselves.

Bunting

Bunting is softly tapping a pitch so that it drops on the infield grass. Often, the main goal of a bunt is to move a runner. This is called a **sacrifice**. However, a good bunt often gets the batter on base too. With practice, anyone can be an excellent bunter.

Bunting begins with a good soft grip, as Katy shows in the photograph at left. Make an imaginary squirt gun with your back hand. Extend your thumb upward. Point your index finger. It will be the gun barrel. Now, pull your index finger as if you were pulling the trigger. You have made a V with the base of your thumb and the fleshy area that extends to the fingers. The bat should rest loosely in the V. Your fingers and thumb are protected by the bat, not wrapped around it.

Loosely grip the handle of the bat with your other hand. This hand should be 12 to 18 inches from the knob. The bat's barrel should point upward. Keep the bat higher than the ball to avoid hitting a pop fly. Move closer to the pitcher in the bat-

ter's box. This increases your chances of a fair, not foul, bunt. A foul bunt is a strike. If you have two strikes and you hit a foul bunt, you are out.

There are two stances for bunting. The pivot stance is the easiest. The hitter stands close to the plate. The hitter pivots on the balls of his or her feet to face the pitcher.

In the square-off stance, the batter steps away from the plate with his or her front foot. Both hips face the pitcher. The batter's feet are more than shoulder-width apart.

Ben, at right, is using the square-off stance. He holds the bat's barrel at the top of the strike zone, over the plate. He brings the bat to the ball by lowering his body, not his hands. Ben lets the ball hit the bat. You can think of "catching" the ball with the bat.

When you practice bunting, pick out a couple of letters from the brand name on your bat. Pick letters that are 3 or 4 inches from the end of the bat. Watch the ball hit those letters when you bunt.

SURGEONS LTD.

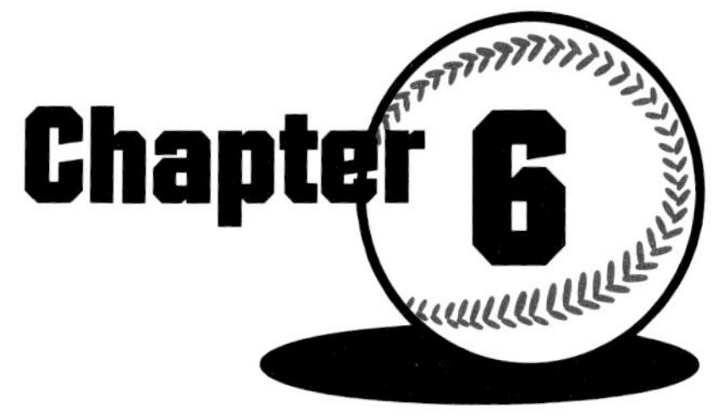

BASERUNNING

Baserunning makes baseball a game of chance and daring. To be a good baserunner, you must first be a good runner. Start with a relaxed body. Keep your feet pointed straight ahead. Run on the balls of your feet with your knees pumping almost to your waist and your heels kicking back to your buttocks. Pump your arms along the sides of your body. Your hands should pump to almost eye level.

Always run as fast as you can. Also, be as daring as you can be. Fielders are more likely to make a mistake if they are worrying about you hustling to a base. If the fielders do make a mistake, be ready to keep running.

After Dave hits the ball and follows through, he drops his bat. Carrying the bat would slow him down. Dave sprints down the first baseline until he gets halfway to first base. Then he runs in foul territory (to the right of the line). If a fielder's throw hits Dave while he is in fair territory, he is out.

Dave runs two or three steps past first base before slowing down. If Dave then turns toward second base, the fielders

may try to tag him out. But if Dave turns toward foul territory and heads back to first base, the fielders can't tag him.

If Dave's hit reaches the outfield, he veers to his right 4 to 6 feet when he is two-thirds of the way to first base. He touches first base with his right foot and pushes off toward second base. Often, coaches near first base and third base will help the baserunners decide when to keep going.

• *Leading Off*

A good lead helps a baserunner advance to the next base, either on a hit or a **stolen base**. Try standing 10 to 15 feet from the base, but don't get put out! Watch the pitcher all the time.

Ben has his right toe on the corner of first base. He is facing second base. Ben takes a 2-foot step with his left foot, then a 2-foot step with his right foot. He turns and faces home plate. Then he takes two 2½-foot shuffle steps toward second base. Don't cross your feet when leading off. Keep your weight on the balls of your feet so it's easy to start running. Ben throws his left arm across his body as he runs to second base.

Ben, the baserunner, is as far from second base as Dave, the second baseman, is.

When you are on second base, you can lead off as far as the shortstop and second baseman are from the bag. For example, the closest fielder in the photograph above is about 15 feet from second base. So the baserunner is leading off about 15 feet. Try to lead off 5 feet behind a straight line from second base to third base. This helps you watch the second baseman and shortstop. Also, you are ready to round third base and sprint for home if there's a hit.

Be careful. If the ball is hit between the shortstop and third baseman, the shortstop could field the ball and make a short throw to third to put you out. When you're on second base, don't run when a ball is hit to your right unless there's a runner on first or you're positive that the ball will reach the outfield. If the ball is hit to your left, sprint for third. The fielder will have a long throw across the infield to put you out.

When leading off third base, as Missy is below, stand 2 feet in foul territory. Missy is as far from the bag as the third baseman is. As the pitch is released, Missy takes two steps toward home plate and leans forward. She's ready to sprint home if the ball gets past the catcher or if it's hit.

Be sure you are in foul territory when you lead off. If a batted ball hits you while you're in foul territory, you're not out. But if you're hit by a batted ball while in fair territory, you're out.

• *Stealing*

When a baserunner moves to the next base without a hit, an error, or a fielder's choice, the baserunner has "stolen" a base. To steal a base, watch the pitcher. Be ready to rush back to the base on the pitcher's first move. Once you know a pitcher's **pickoff move,** you're better prepared to steal.

• *Sliding*

Sooner or later, you will need to **slide**. Sliding into a base in a big cloud of dust is fun. Sliding also helps you to avoid overrunning a base or being tagged out. Wear long, heavy pants when you're learning to slide. Practice on the grass and don't wear your shoes.

Dave starts his slide about 10 feet from the base. He lifts both feet from the ground at the same time. Dave extends his right leg. He bends his left leg and touches the base with his left foot.

CHAMPRO

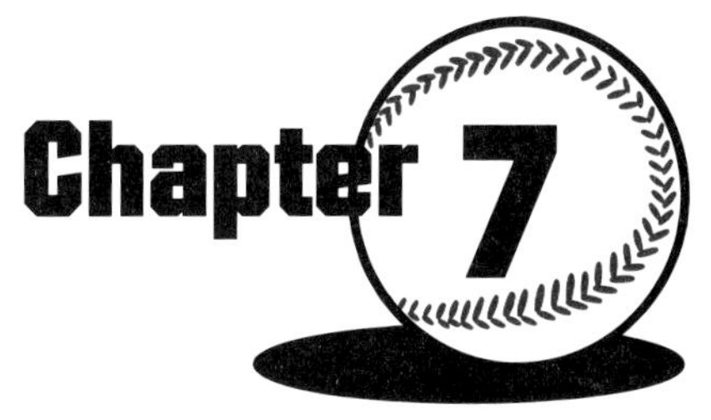

ON THE FIELD

After you have practiced the basic skills, you will want to use those skills in a game. Each position on a baseball team calls for some special talents. But all the players need the fundamentals. If you practice and try hard, you can learn to play different positions.

You will have discouraging days. Sometimes you will walk many batters. You may turn an easy out into a costly error. You may strike out with the bases loaded. Teammates, opponents, coaches, and parents can all add pressure. Don't listen to anyone's negative voice. Have confidence that with practice and effort you will succeed. Have fun!

Pitcher

A pitcher must learn four basic body positions. Practice these motions in front of a mirror. With time, you can master even the positions that are uncomfortable at first.

Jay is demonstrating these positions in the photographs. He's lefthanded. If you're not, pretend you are looking in a mirror. Use the opposite hand or foot that Jay is using.

To grip the ball for a fastball, put your index and middle fingers across the wide seams.

Jay starts his motion with his feet shoulder-width apart. His front foot is 6 inches toward the first baseline. He keeps the ball hidden in his glove. He holds his glove at chest level.

• *Knee to Glove*

Jay lifts his front knee above his waist. His glove is a few inches above his knee. His

head, and his elbow is above his shoulder. This is the *eagle* position.

Jay reaches back with his elbow bent slightly. This coiling of his arm creates more power.

Imagine Dracula raising his cape to hide his fangs. Jay uses that motion with his glove arm as his other arm lifts the ball. Jay lifts his glove about 10 inches away from his front shoulder. His elbow is down.

weight is on the ball of his back foot. His knee is bent, as if he were going to jump. Jay's weight is balanced on both feet. Being balanced gives him his maximum power.

• Eagle to Dracula

Next, Jay takes the ball out of his glove. His palm faces down. His hand is higher than his

• *Pull to Throw*

Now Jay cocks his throwing wrist so that his fingers are on top of the ball and his palm faces up. He pulls his front elbow down toward his hip and steps forward on his front leg. His front foot points directly toward home plate.

As Jay's back leg pushes forward, the front of his body pulls his arm forward. His wrist whips the ball directly toward the catcher's mitt. Jay releases the ball when it is 2 to 3 feet in front of his body.

• *Follow-Through*

Jay pushes off his back leg. As his front side pulls him forward and down, he shifts his weight. He finishes with his back foot even with or slightly ahead of his front foot. His throwing hand finishes near his opposite knee. After his follow-through, Jay gets ready to field any ball hit his way.

Bad Moves

Throwing across your body can hurt your throwing shoulder. If you're right-handed and your front foot lands to the right of an imaginary line from your front shoulder to the target, you're throwing across your body (left of the line for lefthanders). If your front foot steps across your body, your hips and front side can't rotate fully.

To check where your foot lands, make a line in the dirt directly toward your target. Your foot should land on this line.

Catcher

A catcher must be tough and have a strong arm. A catcher also must not mind being hit by the ball or by baserunners.

A catcher uses hand signals to tell the pitcher what pitch to throw. To do this, Andy squats on his heels. Andy's right hand is between his legs. Using his fingers, he signals to the pitcher.

When there is a runner on base, the catcher must quickly throw the ball after a pitch.

Andy spreads his legs and extends his glove toward the pitcher. His throwing hand is behind his back or his glove. After he catches the ball, he brings his arm back into the eagle position. At the same time, he steps toward his target.

Catchers must also block balls that are thrown in the dirt. To do this, Andy falls to his knees with his glove on the ground between his knees. He hunches forward with his shoulders and tucks his chin.

First Base

A first baseman must be able to catch all types of throws. A first baseman doesn't have to be tall, but it is helpful when he or she must stretch to catch a high throw.

For any throw, the first baseman must run to first base as soon as the ball is hit. The first baseman places a foot on the front of the base, then faces the fielder who is making the play. The first baseman's foot stays on the bag. He or she stretches as far as possible to catch the ball as quickly as possible.

Second Base

A second baseman must be able to tag a baserunner. The second baseman must run quickly to the base. He or she must straddle the bag and catch the ball. Then the second baseman sweeps his or her glove down and tags the bag. Hold the ball in your glove with your throwing hand. This way, the runner is tagged out trying to touch the base. If you reach for the runner, he or she may slide underneath or around your tag.

A second baseman also must be able to help make a double play. If the ball is hit to the third-base side of second base, the second baseman runs to the base. Once the second baseman has the ball, he or she throws the ball to the first baseman. If the ball is hit to the first-base side of second base, the second baseman fields the ball. The shortstop covers second base and makes the throw to the first baseman.

Wall Ball

Practice throwing a tennis ball against a flat, smooth surface that leads up to a wall. Steps or a sturdy garage door are good for this practice. Spread your feet wider than your shoulders. Keep your throwing-side foot slightly behind your other foot.

Shortstop

A shortstop fields the ball and backs up other fielders. A shortstop has a big area to cover, so he or she must react quickly.

Third Base

The third baseman needs good hands and a strong arm. A third baseman often must field a bunt. The third baseman runs full-speed to the ball. When he or she reaches it, the third baseman crouches down to catch it. If the ball is not moving, the third baseman picks it up with his or her bare hand. If the ball is moving, the third baseman catches it with both hands. Then, the third baseman steps forward and throws.

Hitting the Cutoff

A cutoff is a fielder who catches a throw and relays the ball to another fielder. Here's an example of a cutoff play. It's illustrated in the diagram below:

There's a runner on second base. The batter lashes a double to the left-center field fence. Jeremy, the center fielder, fields the ball. The shortstop, Ernie, runs halfway into the outfield. Jeremy throws the ball to Ernie.

Ernie catches the ball. He turns and throws to the third baseman, Mike. Mike catches the ball, turns, and throws to the catcher. The catcher tags out the runner. Ernie and Mike were the cutoffs in the play.

When you are the cutoff, give your fielder a good target at which to throw. Be sure you're in a direct line from the fielder to your target.

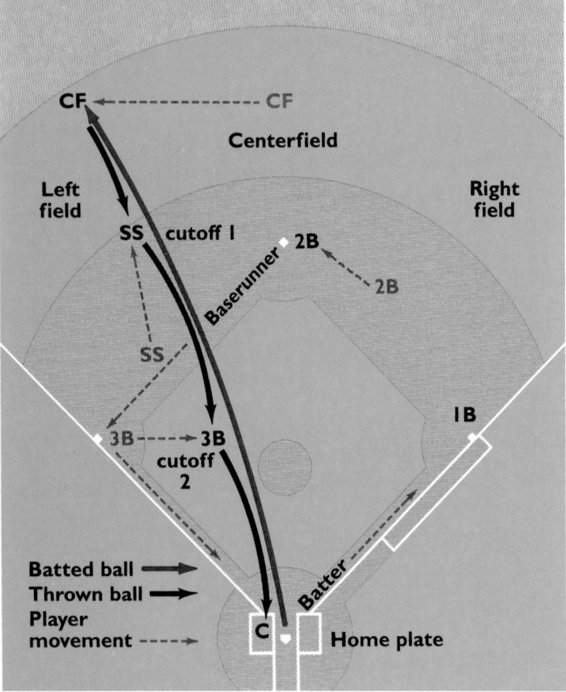

Outfield

Outfielders need to be able to catch fly balls and make long, accurate throws. A centerfielder should be fast because he or she has the most area to cover. A rightfielder should have a strong arm to throw from right field to third base. A leftfielder must be reliable because most balls will be hit to left field.

Millions of people learned to play baseball as children. They grew up playing and watching it. Some of them passed their love of the game of baseball on to their children.

Baseball is called America's game. It's a popular sport in many countries, however. Many people all over the world enjoy playing this exciting sport. Now you can too!

BASEBALL TALK

at bat: An official attempt to hit a pitched ball. Hitting a sacrifice, being walked, or being hit by a pitch doesn't count as an at bat.

ball: A pitch that doesn't pass through the strike zone and at which the batter doesn't swing.

base on balls: A free pass to first base, awarded to a batter who receives four balls before being put out by a strikeout or a fielder. Also called a walk.

batter's box: One of two 4 foot by 6 foot rectangles, 6 inches from both sides of home plate. The batter's boxes are marked with chalk. The batter must have one foot in one of the boxes when hitting the ball.

batting average: The number of hits a batter gets, divided by his or her official at bats (not counting walks or sacrifices), carried to three decimal places. For example, if Dave has 9 at bats and gets 3 hits, his batting average is .333—excellent!

change-up: An intentionally slow pitch that is thrown with the same motion as a fastball to fool the hitter.

curveball: A pitch thrown with a snap and twist of the pitcher's wrist. A right-handed pitcher's curve breaks from right to left; a left-hander's breaks from left to right.

double play: The act of putting out two baserunners on one play. One of the most common double plays occurs when there is a runner on first and the batter hits the ball to the second baseman. The second baseman or shortstop forces out the runner at second and throws to first to put out the batter.

error: A mistake by a fielder that causes a batter or baserunner to reach a base safely.

fastball: A pitch thrown at full speed.

fielder's choice: A decision by a fielder who has fielded a batted ball to throw the ball to a base other than first base in order to put out a runner already on base. The batter isn't credited with a hit even if the play isn't successful.

fly ball: A batted ball that goes high into the air above fair territory.

force-out: A situation in which a baserunner must go to the next base, but the fielder holding the ball touches the base before the baserunner. A force-out, also called a force play, can only happen at first base or when there is a runner on first base.

ground ball: A batted ball that rolls or bounces on the ground. Also called a grounder.

hit: A batted ball that causes the batter to reach base safely without an error, fielder's choice, or interference call.

home run: A batted ball that goes over the fence in fair territory to score a run for the batter's team, once he or she touches all the bases. Runners on base when the ball is hit also score. If there are three runners on base when a home run is hit, it's called a grand slam home run. An inside-the-park home run is a hit that allows the baserunner to touch all the bases before the ball is thrown home. Also called a homer.

inning: A division of the game in which each team has a turn to bat.

line drive: A hard-hit ball that travels on a straight, relatively low path.

lineup: The order in which the members of a team bat. Once the game has started, the lineup can't be changed, although substitutions are allowed. Also called the batting order.

out: The failure of a batter to reach a base safely. A team is allowed three outs in an inning.

pickoff move: A sudden throw from the pitcher or catcher to an infielder to catch a baserunner off base.

pop fly: A batted ball that goes high in the air above the infield.

putout: A play in which a defensive player stops or catches the ball and causes a batter or runner to be out.

sacrifice: A play in which the batter hits the ball and is put out but succeeds in advancing a teammate at least one base. The batter's team must have fewer than two outs.

slide: The action of a baserunner who, to avoid over-running the base or being tagged out, drops to the ground and slides to the base.

stolen base: A base that a baserunner reaches without the benefit of a hit, error, or fielder's choice.

strike: A pitch that passes through the strike zone without being hit or that the batter swings at and misses. Also, a pitch that is hit foul when the batter has fewer than two strikes. A foul bunt is also a strike.

strikeout: An out resulting from a batter being charged with three strikes.

strike zone: The area over home plate between the batter's armpits and the top of the knees. If a pitch passes through this zone, it's a strike.

tag: The action of a fielder in touching a baserunner with the ball in order to put out the baserunner.

FURTHER READING

Galt, Margot Fortunato. *Up to the Plate, The All American Girls Professional Baseball League.* Minneapolis, Minn.: Lerner Publications, 1995.

Jordon, Pat. *Sports Illustrated Pitching: The Keys to Excellence.* New York: Sports Illustrated Books, 1988.

Kindall, Jerry. *Sports Illustrated Baseball: Play the Winning Way.* Lanham, Maryland: Sports Illustrated Books, 1993.

Schmidt, Mike, and Rob Ellis. *The Mike Schmidt Study: Hitting Theory, Skills and Technique.* New York: McGriff & Bell, 1994.

Winfield, Dave, with Eric Swenson. *The Complete Baseball Player.* New York: Avon Books, 1990.

FOR MORE INFORMATION

Babe Ruth Baseball
524½ Hamilton Avenue
Trenton, N.J. 08609

Little League Baseball, Inc.
P.O. Box 3485
Williamsport, PA 17701

National Baseball Congress
Box 1420
Wichita, KS 62201

U.S.A. Baseball
2160 Greenwood Avenue
Trenton, N.J. 08609

INDEX